MOON WISE

HOW TO FIND PEACE AND POWER WITH THE
CYCLE OF THE MOON

AWEN CLEMENT

COPYRIGHT

Title: Moon Wise

First published in 2019

ISBN 9781686737411

Illustration: © Caitlin Noble

For Charli, Tyler, Eleni & Connor

CONTENTS

We were all Moon Wise once.
There was a time when we lived by its
darkness and its light.

We knew when to plant our gardens and when
to harvest our herbs.
We knew when it was time to dance and when
babies would be born.

In time our knowing slipped away, became hidden
in stories and folk tales.
But somewhere within us all, when we see
the moon in the sky,
we feel something stirring within us.

As the moon pulls the tides, so it pulls at us,
pulls at our memory.
We can become Moon Wise once more.

Introduction

A Message From The Author

My name is Awen and I am a lifelong follower of the Pagan spiritual path. Raised by a Pagan mother and a father who was a scholar of myth and folklore, my childhood was woven with story and ceremony and the moon has been a powerful presence in my life for as long as I can remember.

The full moon has always pulled at me. A deep sense of peace always comes to me when I see it riding the horizon. Now as an adult I work as a ceremonialist and a healer and this book is the fruit of years of reading and sitting in circle with teachers from a wide variety of paths. Anyone who has worked with me will know that nearly everything I do will have the essence of the moon within it.

My relationship with the moon fundamentally changed and deepened during my pregnancy with my youngest son in 2013. In the years since that pregnancy I have read everything I can get my hands on about the moon, about the astrology of it, about its connections to menstruation and pregnancy and how it can be used magically and spiritually.

In 2016 I ran a year-long programme called Moon Wise Woman, offering a space to explore the cycle of the moon month to month through creative exercise, meditation and drum journeying and with input from a variety of guest teachers who had their own ways of living and working with the moon.

In 2018 I gave a talk about my concept of the Natal Moon Phase and the moon cycle of the year and the notes from that talk have formed the backbone of this book. I truly believe that knowing about yourself in relation to the phases of the moon can be life changing.

You don't need to be a Pagan to use this book, you don't need to menstruate or have birthed babies. I believe the Natal Moon Phase concept applies to *everyone* and you can work with this book from a purely logical view point or add it to your spiritual work and understanding in whatever way suits you best. This concept can work alongside other practices or understandings you may have around the moon, either through spiritual practice or astrology. This is about how the moon impacts you on a personal level rather than the wider and more general energies that may apply.

These days I live my life from month to month, or should I say moon to moon, based on a deep, personal understanding of my Natal Moon Phase cycle. Everything I do, everything I plan, I stop and check what the moon is doing first. It makes a difference to my work, to my creativity and my family life. It's my wish to share this wisdom with you and hope to make a difference to you too.

PART I

LIVING MOON WISE

Why Understanding the Moon Matters

If I were to ask you, would you know your star sign? Your rising sign? Maybe even your moon sign? But would you know what *phase of the moon* you were born under?

We are all cyclical beings, regardless of our gender, race or culture. The cycle of the moon is the one cycle we can most consistently measure and follow. They say the moon pulls at us the way it pulls at the tides of the ocean, for we are mostly water too.

In these modern times many people use the moon as a magical guide. Our ancestors used it even more closely. They almost certainly used it as a calendar of the year, but actually it was deeper than that. Farming and gardening was once done according to the cycles of the moon and you didn't plant or harvest in certain phases. The phase of the moon is said to make a difference to when you should have medical surgery, when you should cut your hair and more.

Each moon cycle of the year has its own energy and meaning and has importance in regard to what is happening in nature. In many cultures around the world, the different moons of the year have different names, according to what is happening on the land and with birds and animals. Given that we are also a part of nature, not separate from it, it follows that these cycles have a relevance and importance for us too.

Following many years of study and personal practice I have come to understand that we have a personal energy cycle that is in direct relation to the phase the moon was in on the day that we were born. This is your Natal Moon Phase and the corresponding day every month is your personal power day. If we make our way through the year understanding our own personal moon cycle in relation to the moon cycle through the seasons, we have the possibility to live, work and create more powerfully than ever before.

This book is split into two halves. In the first half I outline how to understand and explore your Natal Moon Phase and how you can use that to understand your personal energy cycles and the difference that can make to how you live. In the second half I offer a walk through the year with the moon, offering concepts and ideas for you to explore each month. The idea being that you can use your understanding of your personal connection with the moon in combination with the wider energies of the moon through the year.

Moon Phase Basics

You may already be well informed in your understanding of the cycle of the moon, but on the chance that this book is the first time you've been made aware of it, here is a beginner's guide to the phases of the moon and the language we use around it.

New Moon – when the moon isn't visible at all in the night sky

Waxing Crescent – when the moon is starting its journey towards full and is visible as a thin crescent

First Quarter – the halfway point between New Moon and Full Moon

Waxing Gibbous – when the moon is more than halfway to being full

Full Moon – when the moon is at its biggest and brightest and looks like a perfect circle

Waning Gibbous – when the moon is waning away from full

Third Quarter – the halfway point between Full Moon and New Moon

Waning Crescent – when the moon is completing the cycle and looks like a thin crescent again

Waxing always refers to the time between new moon and full moon and waning the time between full moon and new moon. People may refer to the time of 'dark moon' and they mean the last couple of days immediately before new moon when it is just barely visible in the sky.

In most magical and spiritual models of working with the moon the practices always treat the new moon as the beginning of the cycle and the full moon as the peak of the cycle. So for example new projects or anything around new beginnings should be done around the new moon, anything which needs an energy boost or making big wishes and intentions should be done at the full moon and any magic around releasing or banishing should be done in the dark of the moon.

Many people find this model works for them extremely well, but anecdotally there are plenty of people who don't. My understanding of this is that it's because those people are working at odds to their Natal Moon Phase Cycle, as explained here by Louise.

Louise's Natal Moon Phase is directly on New Moon and she had this to say.

"I had been aware for a while that I was born around the dark moon, but until I chatted with Awen, I never really understood what that meant. Since paying attention I've noticed

that I have more vivid and meaningful dreams around my natal moon. I've also always been drawn to working spiritually and magically during the dark moon too, even though a lot of information points towards working during the full moon. "

There are many journals and digital applications available that you can use to work out what the moon is doing. Some people find that it takes a while to get to grips with which way it's going as at certain points it looks the same shape whether it's waxing or waning. As you become more familiar, you'll be able to see that the shapes are the opposite way around!

The best way to really become familiar with the phases and how the moon cycles is get outside and look for it every day. Sometimes it will be more visible at night and sometimes early in the morning. The more you observe it the more familiar it will become and in time you may not need to look, to know what it is doing.

Becoming Moon Wise

I'm sure it's clear by now that I believe that we are all affected by the moon. Regardless of our gender, our spiritual beliefs or whether we menstruate or not. I believe that our personal power, our energy flow stems from our personal cycle with the moon as it flows from our Natal Moon Phase day. That is to say – the day in the month when the phase of the moon matches the phase it was in on the day that we were born.

I became Moon Wise when I was pregnant with my youngest son. I was doing a lot of work with menstrual and pregnancy magic and cycles and the moon is often connected with this. One of my teachers taught me that when we are not bleeding for any reason, that we can follow the cycle of the moon instead. This works by classing the new moon as day one of the cycle. In this way you use the moon as a way of understanding your cyclical self without menstruation.

For three years, through pregnancy and two years of breastfeeding I charted and tracked myself with the moon, keeping journals and writing regular prayers and intentions through each cycle. But then when my bleed returned, after my little boy weaned, I found that the energy of my menstrual cycle had less impact on me. My personal cycle with the moon was far more relevant and powerful.

Around the same time I started noticing people on social media saying things like - "its full moon but I feel rubbish". The neo-pagan model of working with moon says that full moon is the time of high energy, but a lot of people just weren't feeling it. It prompted me to ask these people, "What's your date of birth?". And, sure enough, nine times out of ten, those people who said that they felt rubbish at full moon were born in the time of the waning moon or close to new moon.

I've tested this theory time and time again over the last few years. The rule has proved to largely be true that people feel their best or their strongest, are most creative and have their highest energy around the time of their Natal Moon Phase and then conversely, they feel at their lowest at the opposing side of the cycle. It's important to note at this point, that it's not enough to only know the general phase of the moon when you were born, it matters to the exact day. i.e. two days before full moon, exactly on third quarter, one day after new moon etc.

The moon is a constant unlike so many of the other seasons and cycles that we might work by. The seasons of nature, the calendar year, the weather, life seasons, menstrual cycles and so on. There is power in all of these cycles and understanding the part they can play in your life is important, as you will see in the second half of this book. But the moon is always there, waxing and waning consistently, cycle after cycle.

My experience has been that by paying attention to what the moon is doing I can manage my life, my work, my children – basically everything - better. I won't say I'm perfect at it, some months I forget to pay attention, it's always a work in progress! But when I do pay attention life is so much easier. I believe the moon influences us all and that we can learn how to work with it to get the best out of life.

The Moon Wise Cycle

In order to help you understand what living in tune with your Natal Moon Cycle looks like, the best thing to do is explain how it works for me.

My Natal Moon Phase, the phase of the moon on the day I was born, is two days before full moon. As the moon arrives at its first quarter phase (waxing) I feel my energy starting to build and it keeps building up to my Natal Moon day. It stays quite strong for a few days afterwards and then as it passes full moon and starts to wane again, it starts to drop away.

So, for those few days around my Natal Moon day I feel full of positive energy; confident, creative and able to get everything done. I've learnt that this is the time to deal with things like difficult phone calls, tedious admin and housework! It's also often a time of high libido and heightened sensuality.

Then in contrast, my low point of the month is in the couple of days before the new moon. I feel tired and slow, I find it hard to be social and out in the world and have to remind myself to be gentler and slower in my activities.

When I remember to pay proper attention it makes a huge difference to my ability to maintain a balance in my energy levels. It makes a difference to my creativity, my business and my ability to be able to support others.

When I've had that space of high energy around the full moon, then I can use that lower time as a space for self-care so that the high time doesn't burn me out completely. Burn out is a familiar thing to many of us in this fast paced, modern world. Following our personal energy cycle with the moon can help us to manage bigger life events and the wider energy of the world better too.

Now, the thing is, my Natal Moon Cycle happens to fit with the traditional model of the energy cycle working to the natural waxing and waning of the moon, so you might doubt what I'm suggesting about the Natal Moon Phase connection. I can only say to you that anecdotally more than a hundred people I have spoken to in the last few years have found that this concept works. Below are some stories of other people's experience of living and working with their Natal Moon Cycle.

Emma's Natal Moon Phase is a couple of days after the new moon and this is what she said to me about her experience of noticing her personal energy in relation to it.

> *"I absolutely feel more creative at the new moon, very inspired, sometimes a little too wired in fact. The full moon I tend to be exhausted and overwhelmed or want to retreat."*

Of course not everyone is conveniently born around the full or new moon, you may have been born anywhere in between them, on the waxing or waning side. The rule still holds, your Natal Moon Phase day will still be the peak of your personal cycle and the Opposing Phase the lower side. It's just that it may not be so obvious visually speaking where the moon is in the cycle until you get more familiar with it.

Nikki's Natal Moon Phase is the day before full moon and this is what she had to say.

"I always find full moons very relaxing and wondrous. I know generally full moons are supposed to make people go crazy but I always wondered why they had the opposite effect on me until I found out it was the phase I was born under. With regards to dark moon, I always feel slightly on edge about it as I am not a fan of total darkness unless I am sleeping!"

Deniz was born in the dark of the moon and she said this

"I am much more comfortable around the dark moon. Steadier and grounded and calm. Full moon I rather hide away from, it feels a rather disruptive energy. I love catching a glimpse of full moons but resist the pull to be too active"

However it is also worth noting that occasionally there are people who don't find that they fit the Natal Moon Phase Cycle. It's rare, but the reality is that given the billions of people there are on the planet, not everyone is going to fit neatly into any concept or theory. There will always be people on the edges. This is why it is important to chart your own personal cycle.

Stephanie was born exactly on full moon and this is what she told me

> "If I'm not very careful at full moon I often feel like I can feel the whole world, and it's sad and hopeless and vast. I mean not just all the people but the land and the trees; it's overwhelming. Most of the time on a new moon I feel like I could literally change the whole world, I can talk to anyone, solve anything, nothing bothers me and I feel lighter."

CHARTING YOUR MOON WISE CYCLE

The first thing to do of course, is find out what your Natal Moon Phase day is. But you do need to know to the exact day i.e. two days before new moon, a day after full moon etc. Then you also need to work out what your opposing phase is as well. An easy way to do this is to use a visual moon cycle chart, with the phases laid out in a circle. Look at where your Natal Moon Phase is on the chart and then look at which phase is directly opposite it on the circle. There are links to charts to help you with this at the end of the book.

The way then to understand your personal moon cycle is to practice cycle charting. There are a number of ways of charting and the simplest is probably by using a diary. Some diaries even have the phases of the moon marked on each day or at least new moon and full moon. Find a way of coding your Natal Moon Phase day, I use a little star symbol for mine. Also code the opposing day in the cycle, I use a little sad face. I copy this code to my main work/life diary too!

At the end of each day, make notes on some of the following, being as brief or in depth as you feel you need. This isn't meant to be a full journaling practice, though it will work well alongside.

Reflect on the day that's been and how you have felt. What has your energy been like? Have you got a lot done or have you found it really hard? Have you been tired or restless or wired and buzzy? Did you sleep well the previous night? How's your libido? What are your emotions doing? How has your creativity been? Have you noticed any physical sensations? Think about what you want to know and understand about yourself in relation to your moon cycle. Make notes on anything that feels relevant, you can tweak it as you go along.

It's best to chart for at least three months, so that you can look for patterns. If the Natal Moon theory is correct, you should see over the course of the months that your energy rises around your Natal Moon Phase and falls away again at the opposing phase. You may notice other peaks and troughs too.

You may find that it does shift a little bit. The moon cycle is roughly 29 and a half days, some months at 29 and a quarter some 29 and three quarters. So there is a little bit of movement, a little bit of shifting that needs to be accounted for. But I would expect the overall wave of energy through your cycle to go up and down in roughly the same places each month.

It's important to say to also be aware of any bigger events that may be happening in your life as you work with this. Anything that is causing unusual amounts of stress, joy, excitement, grief etc. will skew how your chart looks. i.e. you might be feeling great because you just got a promotion or your partner proposed, even though you're in the lower side of your energy cycle, or you've just had a bereavement or some other upheaval when you're around your Natal Moon Phase day. Physical health matters and any relevant hormone cycles will make a difference too. This is another reason why you should chart over a period of months, so as to have a wider view of the cycle over time, not just a brief snapshot.

It's not to say that you will always feel amazing on your Natal Moon Phase day or that you will feel absolutely dreadful on your opposing phase, it will always be a reflection of you and your state of mind and what is happening in your life. But you may notice that it amplifies things, so negative things or being burnt out is harder at the opposing point in your cycle and positive events will have more impact around your Natal Moon Phase. By charting you will be able to see where this is true.

Once you have some months of charting done you can then start to use this understanding to be able to manage your life better. You'll be able to choose those days of the month when you know it feels good to be sociable, the days that will be good to be out there doing face to face business. If you're writing or painting or creating then you can know when to leave space in the diary for it and when it's less likely to flow well.

And vice versa that you know, in your lower side of the cycle that you're giving yourself space to be in that lower energy. To be nourishing yourself and treating yourself kindly in that space and not putting extra pressure on yourself. You can give yourself permission to let go of work or creativity or being sociable, knowing that in not too long your energy will come back up again.

This is going to be a curiosity to some people who may have spent years following the more traditional, albeit modern, way of working with the moon from new moon to new moon. If that works for you, that's brilliant. But I would still encourage you to have a go at charting yourself in relation to your Natal Moon Phase. Don't feel that you have to stop any of your practices, but see if there is a difference, experiment a bit and see what happens.

I have found that aligning my spiritual and magical practices to my personal cycle with the moon to be much more effective than the traditional model. We are all unique beings, with a unique relationship with the moon. The phase of the moon on the day you arrived onto this planet is your personal power day – use it!

Moon Wise Work and Business

We all have those days where we just aren't feeling it, we don't want to get out of bed and head for work, or if we're self-employed it feels like pulling teeth to get anything done. Now we may not have much choice about whether we turn up for work or not, but by understanding our Natal Moon Cycle, we can learn when we need to be kinder to ourselves as it relates to our working life or running a business.

So for me, I don't schedule meetings when I am coming up to my Opposing Phase, I often find it difficult to deal with people or to communicate clearly at this time. Obviously sometimes it can't be avoided, but wherever possible I arrange meetings during the waxing moon in the run up to my Natal Moon Phase day.

If I'm starting a new project, launching something or starting a new marketing campaign I do it around my Natal Moon Phase day. I'm more energised and more engaged with what I'm doing and it's more likely to go well. I use the lower side of the cycle for the planning so that everything is good to go when the high side of the cycle comes round.

It can also be valuable to know the Natal Moon Phase of people you work with, so if you're going to be working on a project together, you will know how to manage the energy flow between you if you don't have a similar phase. That said, sometimes combinations of moon phases can work really well in projects as it helps to maintain a balance across a period of time. It's also said that new moon people are good at getting things started, full moon people are full of ideas and dark moon people are good for getting things completed. Something to experiment with perhaps!

FAMILY AND RELATIONSHIPS

It can be useful to find out what the Natal Moon Phase day is for your family members and loved ones. For any loved ones you live with or people that you spend a lot of time with it can really help to understand the dynamics at play. It can show up why you sometimes end up clashing with people. If you're in your opposing phase and that collides with somebody else's opposing phase and you're both feeling low, it can make things really difficult. Or if you're in your low phase and somebody else is in their high phase, you can find them too much and find them overwhelming.

I've noticed that when my children are being their most difficult it can be because they are in their Opposing Phase, or they are in their Natal Moon time and are wired up and don't sleep so well. It doesn't mean we shouldn't maintain our normal boundaries, but that level of understanding of what is going on can some-times mean that situations don't escalate and become more difficult than necessary. You can work out ways to calm every one down and make the best of what is happening.

By understanding how your energy cycle fits with others you can learn when you need to make space to either be around people or not be around people. I find it ex-tremely difficult to be sociable when I'm at my Opposing Phase, so I don't arrange to see friends or big family gatherings then if I can help it. I also pay atten-tion to where the children and I are in our cycles if we've been invited to things like birthday parties, which al-ready have a lot of energy and stimulation around them.

CREATIVITY

I've definitely noticed a relationship between my Natal Moon Phase and my creativity, which for me is ex-pressed through writing and crafts such as woodwork. In fact I am literally writing this paragraph on the night of my Natal Moon Phase! As you saw from some of the stories earlier in the book, people like Emma also know there is a correlation between the moon and their crea-tive practice.

What if your writers block is actually that you're in your Opposing Phase? Notice what the moon is doing when that amazing painting or piece of craft work seems to just suddenly flow and come into being without effort. Instead of trying to force your creativity to come through no matter what, see if you can find a rhythm that works for you in relationship to your moon cycle.

Menstruation and Fertility

There is already a lot of writing and other work available around working with the moon and its relationship to the menstrual cycle, fertility and child birth. For me there are two things I want to say about it here in relationship to what I am discussing in this book, but I have put resources in the Appendix if this is something you want to explore more. I'm deliberately not going too deeply into it here, because this text is intended to be accessible to everyone but this information won't be relevant for everyone.

Firstly, I think that the moon cycle is the foundational layer of our energy cycle. I know that not everyone will agree with me on this, but because of my experience of exploring this when I wasn't menstruating first, I know that I am more driven by the energy of the moon than by my hormones. But that said, if you have a menstrual cycle you should include it in your charting because like other wider life events, it will have an impact and an influence on your energy. You will find that depending on your cycle length, it will change position in the moon cycle across the course of the year.

Secondly, there is some evidence that some people may ovulate on their Natal Moon Phase day, separately from when they would expect to ovulate according to their menstrual cycle. So if you are wanting to become pregnant or wishing to avoid it, this may be something to bear in mind. Using the resources later in the book as mentioned it is possible to get really deeply into all the different signals the body gives around ovulation, if you want to understand more about this.

PART 2

THE MOON WISE YEAR

MOON WISE CYCLE OF THE YEAR

In this second half of the book we are going to explore the moon across the calendar year. Across different cultures and countries the full moons of each month have different names.

These names are connected to the seasons, the weather and community activity that may be happening at that time of year and are specific to the geography they relate to. This is why you will see that some months have the same name as the preceding or following months.

Bear in mind that due to the moon cycle being 29 and a half days, it doesn't neatly fit into the calendar months and in some years you may find there are two full moons or two new moons in a month, with the second ones being known as Blue Moon and Black Moon respectively.

Each of the moons of the year has its own energy, its own purpose, focus and attributes. As you travel through the year use the notes provided here to guide you on your journey with each moon cycle.

It's worth noting that this book and its guidance comes from a Northern Hemisphere centric perspective because that is where I live and work. If you live in the Southern Hemisphere you may find the following pages don't fit for you. However through awareness and cycle charting you may find your own yearly map of the moon and the seasons.

I invite you to consider how powerful it could be to combine the knowledge of your Natal Moon Cycle, with the energy of each moon cycle of the year and how you can apply that to your life.

As you work through the material and some of the suggested exercises maintain an awareness of where you are in your Natal Moon Cycle, experiment with things and see if the outcome is different at different times of the month and across different times of the year.

Traditionally speaking each named moon cycle begins with the new moon, peaking at the full moon and then waning down till the next cycle starts with the next new moon. Your Natal Moon Cycle may influence how you feel about it.

I don't think there is a right or wrong way, follow your instincts and see what you observe through your cycle charting and other practices in relationship to this wider information about the moons cycle through the year.

I would suggest the way to work with this section of the book would be to keep a notebook or diary and write down your insights through each cycle. This would be alongside or in addition to your cycle charting. You may also wish to record any actions you take or make use of the creative prompts at the end of each section.

Not only do we have a personal energetic relationship with the moon, but many of us recognise seasonal ups and downs within ourselves too. See what you notice on all levels as you travel through the year.

THE JANUARY MOON

Quiet Moon, Frost Moon, Cold Moon, Wolf Moon,
Old Moon, Rowan Moon

For the cycle of the January moon I invite you to focus on Protection. What does the energy of Protection mean for you? The energy flow of the January moon is slow and conservative, of new life and energy gently beginning below the surface

January

January is the soft, subtle, quiet time just as the earth starts to ready itself for the Spring. Deep within the land the energy is gently starting to rise. First shoots and buds may be showing themselves and yet there are still frosty mornings and the light falls away early. The air is sharp and our instincts tell us it is time to rest yet, to wait, to bide our time.

In generations past this time was still unsafe, the weather could still be vicious and wolves and other predators were still abroad looking for a meal. So this is an excellent time to make a quiet space for self-reflection, to review your goals and plans. To prepare the ground ready for the creativity that will want to burst to life with the Spring. Is everything safe and ready for the New Year to come?

What no longer serves you? What do you need to release or let go of to make ready for the new? What has come with you through the Winter that needs to be cleared away ready for the Spring?

But also what are you grateful for? What is there to keep with you, ready to be nurtured into something more?

What areas of your life need attention or protection at this turn of the calendar year? Is there anything that doesn't feel safe?

Protection means different things to different people. Protection might mean energy work, it might be cleansing physical spaces and objects. It might be the creation of an energetic circle around you and your home.

Or perhaps it's more literal and practical things that need attention in your life. Checking smoke alarms and door locks, having your car serviced to make sure it's safe. It might be that you need to check in on your people, friends and family, is everyone doing ok? Does anyone need help?

January is a good time to refresh and renew those things which protect us and keep us and our loved ones safe as we travel into the coming year. As we look ahead to the time when we will want to plant the seeds of our intentions, how do we need to prepare the ground both internally and externally?

Protection

Protection of the Home

Checking alarms and locks, hang hag stones at entrance ways, hang a Green Man or Green Woman at the front door, and sweep out negative energies with a besom.

Protection of Your Community

Donating money or volunteering time to charities that protect the vulnerable, litter picking in green spaces, feeding birds and wild animals in need during the Winter, helping elderly friends and neighbours

Energetic Protection

Start a daily practice, either on waking or falling asleep. Visualise yourself in a bubble of light that starts at the centre of yourself and grows outwards. You can stop just beyond yourself or keep going until it enfolds your home and family within.

Write/Journal/Paint

I remember....

I feel safe when....

What does 'home' mean to you...?

THE FEBRUARY MOON

Quickening Moon, Wild Moon, Snow Moon, Ice Moon, Storm Moon, Hunger Moon, Horning Moon

For the cycle of the February moon I invite you to focus on Responsibility. What does the energy of Responsibility mean for you? The energy flow of the February moon is of life quickening in the earth like the babe in the womb, it's gentle yet, but it's getting stronger day by day

February

February and the earth is quickening, there is a sense of urgency in the energy as we move past Imbolc. There is a restlessness, an intensity, an urgency. We are waking up from Winter. There is a need to move and change, there may be feelings of uncertainty.

The light is lasting a little longer, the air is growing a little warmer. This is a good time for planning, for looking forwards towards the future. What seeds can you plant now? What small actions and changes can you make? Following on from the preparation you did during the last moon.

This can be an exciting time but it can also be difficult, you may be feeling pulled in many different directions and unsure which way to go. You may also still be feeling a little slow from the Winter, so there is a resistance to the pulling that leaves us feeling unsettled.

Responsibility as a concept can feel quite a heavy burden. But responsibility can be a conscious choice, it can be a state of power. To choose to actively take responsibility for yourself, your actions, behaviours and your place in the world.

If we do what we can to be responsible for the planet and our part in living on it, this then feeds our communities and our families and the future generations. It's an ongoing positive feedback loop.

As an example, shopping can be a spiritual act, it can be an act of power. Choosing where you buy things from is a responsible act for your community. When we take responsibility for those choices is it a spiritual act.

The only journey we are responsible for is our own. Don't feel that you have to be responsible for anyone else. You can't change people, you can't change circumstances and you can't change events. But you can change your response and reaction to it.

What small changes could you make that will make a big difference in the long term?

How can you make responsibility a conscious choice in your life? An act of power? How will you be responsible for creating your future, for creating how you want to feel?

Responsibility

Responsibility for Self

It is important to recognise that only we are responsible for our journey. We can't change people or circumstances, but we can change our responses to them. We must take responsibility for ourselves, for our choices, our behaviour, our actions; past, present and future.

Responsibility for Community

We each have a role to play within our communities, whether that is just our immediate family or wider circles at work, school and beyond. We each do our part to keep these pieces of our communities' safe, largely by being responsible for ourselves. Each feeds the other. You are not responsible for anyone's journey but your own.

Responsibility for Planet

We all have a responsibility to the planet. By taking care of ourselves, by taking care of our communities, we take care of the Earth. But more than that we can take a more direct responsibility by being conscious of our choices in shopping and consumption, where are you putting your money?

WRITE/JOURNAL/PAINT

I know....

I feel powerful when....

What does 'responsibility' mean to you...?

THE MARCH MOON

Seed Moon, Crow Moon, Plough Moon, Sap Moon,
Worm Moon, Crust Moon, Storm Moon,
Moon of Winds

For the cycle of the March moon I invite you to focus
on Potential. What does the energy of Potential mean
for you? The energy flow of the March moon is rising
strongly, full of potential and fertility, on the edge of
bursting into bloom

March

March and the earth is moving quickly now, plants and trees are bursting into life, birds and animals are bearing young. The crows call to signal Winter is over. Everything is bright and fizzing and anything feels possible. This is a time of great potential. Who knows what each seed is going to do?

Potential and the concept of the seed can mean many things. It can mean fertility, which may mean wanting to create new life or it may mean creativity and new projects. It may mean abundance and prosperity, or the growth of money and success in our lives, something that people often battle with.

It might be about personal growth or spiritual growth. How may we grow and change as a person? How can we deepen our connection with land and spirit?

Your energy may be high now as you feel the energy in the land rising and the hours of daylight increase as we move to the equinox. This is also a time to be thinking about where your life needs balance. Are you putting too much energy into one area of your life and neglecting others?

Potential is about what we are capable of. Fulfilling our potential, or not. That raw fibre, blank canvas, pure form that anything is possible. The only thing that ever stops us from doing anything is ourselves, and it's usually fear that holds us back.

When we are thinking about potential and growth and what we want to see come to fruit and life in our lives, we need to consider whether our soil is prepared. Are we tending to ourselves, to the garden that is our life? Are we paying attention to those things that we need to support us to achieve what we want?

Every little thing we do counts. Every little seed. Every little bit of love and attention you give to the things you want to grow, matter. We don't expect a plant or tree to grow overnight. We need to nurture and feed whatever we are planting or growing, whether that's within ourselves or in our literal gardens. We know that it all takes time, we need to give it love, attendance and nurturance.

We often lose sight of giving that love and attention, it's easily done we live busy lives. We forget to tend those things which are important, especially those things within ourselves.

Where are you not fulfilling your potential? What is holding you back? Let the light of this Seed Moon bring you strength and inspiration to meet it all head on and bring it all to life as we move onward in the year.

POTENTIAL

SPRING CLEANING

Give your physical spaces a good clean and clear. Get rid of unnecessary clutter, tend to the areas where you spend a lot of time. Create a place for your creative work if you don't have one.

START A DAILY PRACTICE.

It might be journaling, which doesn't have to be pages and pages, it can be just a few lines. It might be a sketch or a photograph taken every day. It might be a daily action towards your business goals. You choose what to do, but commit to doing it every day. Nurture those seeds into something more.

KEEP AN IDEAS BOOK

Keep a small notebook on or about your person all the time. If you see something, hear something, read something, watch something which creates a spark in you, write it down! Make some notes, draw a sketch. If not a notebook you could use your mobile phone, which would even allow you to record audio or video.

WRITE/JOURNAL/PAINT

I see....

I feel strong when....

What does 'purpose' mean to you...?

THE APRIL MOON

Growing Moon, Pink Moon, Egg Moon, Grass Moon,
Budding Moon, Seed Moon, Planting Moon

For the cycle of the April moon I invite you to focus on
Creativity. What does the energy of Creativity mean for
you? The energy flow of the April moon is exuberant,
in full bloom and making things happen.

April

April and everything is starting to bloom, showing signs of new growth. The Cherry trees will put out blossom during this month, transient beauty that will vanish on the breeze after a week or two. We're getting more days of blue skies and there is warmth to the sunshine. The butterflies and the bees are awake and moving, everything is feeling full on. The perfect time to be really juicy and creative, bringing forth projects, giving forth energy into things.

Just remember to be mindful of your energy, it's easy to get over enthusiastic and burn out! Follow the flow of the days, be they warm and buzzing or cooler and quiet. Listen to your inner self about how it wants to be in this time. When we follow our inner flow, our creative self is more able to come through, without pressure or being forced.

On those quieter days, nourish yourself with books and images, feed your mind and spirit so that when your energy rises again there is fuel for your creative self and practice. Everyone is creative in some way, shape or form. Creativity is a natural human state and it doesn't have to mean writing or art. Creative thought goes into everything we do.

There is so much fear around creativity and fear can really block us and hold us back in all areas of our lives. Let go of your attachment to the outcome of what you do and just do it for yourself for the joy and pleasure of it.

If you do anything creative that you want to put out into the world, to earn a living, you may have big fears around it. What will people think? Will anybody like it? Will anybody buy it? These thoughts and fears can prevent it from ever happening or certainly make it a much harder process.

One of the best things I have found that has helped me stop being in a constant battle with my fear around my creativity is to stay curious and to play. To not give myself to long to stop and think about it, just have a go, try something new, play around with no end purpose in mind.

A time of growth and exuberance, the sun is getting warmer, bees are waking and the birds are shouting to everyone who will listen. Now is a time to take that leap, make that change, and commit to something new. The odds are stacked in your favour, what are you waiting for? What is holding you back? Gather your courage and your trust – jump!

What is growing for you now, what has sprouted since the March Moon? What do you want to grow? How can you tend and nurture it? What do you want to be harvesting down the line?

CREATIVITY

PLAY

Give yourself permission to play, with thread, with paint, with words, with mud! Get out with the kids, play let's pretend, remember how easy it was to create before being an adult took over. Let go of any attachment to outcome and just enjoy it.

YOU TIME

Commit to giving yourself regular you time to feed your creative self. In the busy world of work and family and life, it can be hard to allow ourselves time to just be. Feed yourself with a trip to a café with a notebook, a visit to the museum or library, go to the theatre or the movies. Feed yourself with something different than your usual day to day.

FIND OTHERS

If creating by yourself feels really hard, no matter how much you might want to, find a group to join. There are groups for every creative endeavour to be found, online or in person. Creating with others is such a joy and the commitment to being part of a group, helps you commit to your creative practice.

WRITE/JOURNAL/PAINT

I am....

I feel brave when....

What does 'wildness' mean to you...?

THE MAY MOON

Merry Moon, Mothers Moon, Bright Moon,
Flower Moon, Milk Moon, Planting Moon

For the cycle of the May moon I invite you to focus on
Celebration. What does the energy of Celebration
mean for you? The energy flow of the May moon is
joyful and abundant and full of strong growth

MAY

The land is joyous and in full bloom, colour everywhere, trees are exploding, everything is coming to life. Even in the city the volume has gone up. Bird song is louder and there are more small animals around. This time is a big celebration of life. This time gives us space to reflect on what we can celebrate in our lives.

It's easy to lose sight of what is good and worthy of celebration, even very small things. It can't be denied we're in an intense space and time in the world. It's easy to miss the good stuff, to miss what could be celebrated.

What is sprouting now from the metaphorical seeds you have planted? Are you remembering to nurture it? Will you be harvesting in the Autumn? Can you make the most of this joyous energy of growth? Review where you are and give it some attention, some love, some nurturing.

A time for celebrating connections with friends, family and partners. The weather is starting to come good, have barbecues or picnics, invite family and friends round. What is that but a celebration of the land with our people? You might not be consciously aware that this is what you are doing. It may be a throwback historically as we feel the lifting of Winter. Those who couldn't travel in poor weather, could come when the weather and the light improved.

Celebrate the abundance and waking of the land for it can be all too fleeting. When solstice comes, the light changes and starts the slow turn towards Autumn again. So you have to make the most of it. Try and remember to celebrate as much as possible, to celebrate the small stuff not just the big stuff. Make the most of this energy while we have it, use it to fuel yourself and your projects towards a strong Autumn harvest.

The earth is wide awake and in full growth, joyful abundance, plants and trees reaching to the sky and drinking in sun and rain. It is a time for celebration, for acknowledging all that is good and growing in our loves. A time for gratitude.

Give some attention to any seeds of intention you planted earlier in the year, give them some love and nurture. Tune in to this time of growth and abundance to support your wishes and dreams.

Celebrate love and family, make time for play and joy with them. Look to little children, be in the moment as they are and revel in their small joys and abundance of love. Like the plants and the trees, drink in every drop and celebrate every small joy.

Celebration

Share the Love

We don't celebrate one another enough. We should be holding and celebrating each other in our stories, not challenging each other. Boost people up just because, not only when they are being negative about themselves. When was the last time you told someone they're awesome, for no reason other than the fact that they are?

Throw a Party

Don't wait for a special occasion, life is the occasion and every day should be celebrated. It's not easy being human and the world is chaotic. Get all your favourite people together and have a party. Eat your favourite foods and dance your socks off, celebrate being alive with every part of your being.

Dance

Go to a club, go to your kids disco, go to that live music session at the local pub or stick something on your headphones and turn it up loud. Move your body for the joy of it. Let rip, let go and don't care who is looking. Get out of your head and into your body.

WRITE/JOURNAL/PAINT

I celebrate....

I feel joyful when....

What does 'abundance' mean to you...?

THE JUNE MOON

Mead Moon, Honey Moon, Moon of Horses,
Strawberry Moon, Rose Moon, Strong Sun Moon,
Lovers Moon

For the cycle of the June moon I invite you to focus on Exploration. What does the energy of Exploration mean for you? The energy flow of the June moon is golden, powerful and abundant, it is resting at the peak and seeking to protect and strengthen

JUNE

This is a strong, powerful, liminal time. The energy is big and ripe, a time to use it or lose it. With the solstice close by this is a time of balance. The turn of the year, the turn towards Autumn, towards the harvest and then ultimately to Winter. A time of reflection of the light and dark within ourselves and the light and dark within the land.

It is important to acknowledge the dark sides of ourselves and to not see it as negative. Can you see your dark side as powerful? Find safe and comfortable ways to explore it, for there is hidden power and energy to be found here.

This is a good time for releasing, for leaving behind things in the previous six months of the year and thinking about what you don't want to carry forward into the darker months. A time for decision making and setting strong intentions. A time to be joyful, to celebrate and honour all that is good in your life.

Exploring requires a certain amount of courage, even if only internally. A willingness to look for the new or conversely to dig deep into the past, into memory. What would you like to explore if you felt brave enough?

Are you willing to explore the expanse of your creative self? Are you willing to throw all the skeletons out of the cupboard? Where have you been unwilling to look? What dark and dusty corners need to have a light shone upon them?

Summer days are a time of fire, a time of transformation, of transmutation. A time to seek to make change. Create yourself a map based on ambition, resolution, intellect, charisma, leadership and understanding. Use your map to explore your way to being the fullest and most whole self that you could be.

Lazy Summer days, everything is lush and green, thunder storms roll through the skies. A time to dream, a time for inner vision, what do you see? What do you hear? What do you feel?

Look back, what have the last six months brought to you? What is blooming? What needs nurturing? What needs releasing?

Look forwards, what is coming? What do you wish for? Where do you need to make space to allow more growth?

It's a time of creation, of finding balance between our physical and spiritual selves. Bringing through the truth of our sacred selves.

Exploration

Find New Places

Choose somewhere new to walk, take a bus or train to somewhere you have never been before, turn right where you would usually go left. Get out of your comfort zone and go exploring. I'm willing to bet that even in an area that you think you know really well, you'll find something new.

Talk

Have a conversation with older members of your family and ask them to tell you their stories. Explore your family history, explore your roots. What can you learn about yourself from these stories? It doesn't just have to be your family members either, speak to older neighbours or members of your community.

Maps

Get hold of some map books, either of your local area or somewhere you would like to get to know. Look for familiar places, look for unusual landmarks. Learn the codes for all the different things hidden on the page.

WRITE/JOURNAL/PAINT

I want to explore....

I feel connected when....

What does 'magic' mean to you...?

THE JULY MOON

Blessing Moon, Oak Moon, Thunder Moon, Hay Moon,
Meadow Moon, Full Buck Moon, Moon of Claiming

For the cycle of the July moon I invite you to focus on
Recharging. What does the energy of Recharging
mean for you? The energy flow of the July moon is
deep and lazy, restful and bountiful, a time for dream-
ing and divination.

JULY

In this space of hot, lazy Summer days there is a need to be still and quiet and restful. We have a tendency to just keep going and it can be really hard to rein that back and just slow down.

These Summer months are meant to be quieter. We aren't designed to function at top speed in the heat and yet thanks to the wonders of modern technology we have air conditioning in our cars and homes and offices in order to be able to keep going, regardless of what the weather is doing.

Gone are the days when the Summer weeks were the time when the children were off school and helping to get the harvest in while the weather was good. When you would have done the work in the cooler parts of the day and then when it got hot you would have gone and napped or played around in the river.

We don't live in that way on the land anymore. Instead, we've traded it for this modern, technological life, where we live amongst the concrete. Where we can drop the temperature down crazily low so that we can keep going until we fall over.

What are the ways you can take time to recharge, to refill? It's going to look different for everybody. It might be about making time and space for physical rest. It might be about different ways of filling your personal cup.

Perhaps you're not finding time to create? Time to paint, to sing, to make music, to dance. What would filling your creative cup look like for you?

Perhaps you need to take time to fill your love cup and you need to spend time with a partner. Perhaps you've become a little disconnected in the rush of life, with family or children. Maybe you just need to love on yourself, good old self love, looking after you how you feel, your inner self, your inner child.

There are always going to be things that need to be taken care of; children, family, business, work, so it isn't always possible to stop completely. But perhaps around the edges of all these things we can pause and check in with ourselves.

When we are still, when we find our centre, our dreams and intentions come clearer, the paths we need to take to achieve them show themselves. If we are depleted, if our cup is empty then the way is murky and unclear. We have nothing to offer, nothing to give. Consider what would you be capable of if all of your needs were being met? Find peace in the Summer warmth, count your blessings and know that all is well

Recharging

Rest

What does rest mean to you? It isn't always about laying down for a nap. Write yourself a list of things which you find restful, see if you can think of 5 or maybe more. Pin it up somewhere so that you notice it when your cup's running low and use one of your restful things to fill you back up.

Time In Nature

We forget that we are wild, natural beings. We weren't made to live in concrete boxes with artificial light and constant noise around us. One of the best ways to recharge is to get out in nature, take a walk, dangle your feet in fresh water and feel the sun on your skin. Find the nearest tree and hang out.

Ask For Help

I don't know anyone who is good at this! We can be our own worst enemies and struggle on pretending everything is fine. Don't get so depleted that everything becomes impossible. Ask for help, work out what you really need. Free or paid, there is help to found for absolutely everything, you just need to ask.

Write/Journal/Paint

I don't remember....

I am recharged when....

What does 'blessing' mean to you...?

THE AUGUST MOON

Corn Moon, Sturgeon Moon, Green Corn Moon,
Grain Moon, Red Moon, Barley Moon, Wort Moon

For the cycle of the August moon I invite you to focus
on Balance. What does the energy of Balance mean for
you? The energy flow of the August moon is that of
harvest time, of gathering in, of appreciation and gratitude for abundance. The time of starting preparations
for Winter.

August

Here now is the time of the grain harvest, if you drive through the countryside during this time of year you will see the big machines gathering it in if the weather has been good and dry. This is the time for noticing where there is abundance in your life and being grateful for it. What harvest are you bringing in? Is it what you were expecting?

Even though the year is turning and the energy is winding down, it is very easy to still feel like you're meant to be going at full tilt and to buy into the system that says you should always be doing more. Trying harder, hustling harder, even though that isn't the energy of this time.

The risk is that a lot of us don't slow down. Everyone has a busy life and it's very easy to overload and lose our balance. Often we want things to be different but we can't see how to change it, we don't know what to do, so we don't do anything. But if we do nothing, then nothing changes.

The farmer and the harvest are a good analogy for finding balance. The basic principle of farming is to prepare the ground, plant the seed and look after the seed. After that, the farmer has to just trust. He has to hope and trust that the weather will be on his side. That there will be the right balance of warmth and rain to make his crop grow. That when the time comes that there will be enough good weather to bring the harvest in at the right time.

The farmer lives in a place of balance between hope and fear, but he always does the work. He's got no way of knowing whether that harvest is going to come true or not but he's got to try because it matters for his family and his community.

So for those of you who are looking for change, who want to change the balance of your lives. Make the small actions and combine them with a healthy dose of trust.

The corn harvest is coming in and we start the slow turn toward the Winter. Over the coming months we will call in, gather in all that we need to sustain us through the cold and the dark.

What are you harvesting? Did your Spring seeds bear fruit? Do some things still need some attention and nurturing before you claim them?

Life is always a balancing act - hopes and fears, joys and sorrows, illness and health – it is always a work in progress. What can you do, right here, right now to bring a deeper balance to your life? What do you need from the land, from your soul, to achieve all that you dream and desire?

Balance

Time Off

So many of us go at flat out all the time. We tell ourselves that our weekend at home is time off. But often it is fuller than our working days. Treat yourself to a day or an hour to do exactly as you please.

Daydreaming

Is your mind is busy all the time? Constant thoughts, to do lists and worries taking up your time when you're not focused on a particular task? It does the mind good to daydream, to just be allowed to drift without purpose. Make space to daydream as often as possible.

Make a Plan

Are you in a place where you aren't sure what to do next or how to get to the goal you are holding in your heart? Write out all the things on your mind, write out your goals and then work out what action steps you might need to take to make them happen. Make a plan and commit to taking steps towards your dreams.

WRITE/JOURNAL/PAINT

I create....

I feel balanced when....

What are your hopes...? What are your fears...?

THE SEPTEMBER MOON

Harvest moon, Corn moon, Barley moon,
Singing moon, Fruit moon, Wine moon, Blood moon

For the cycle of the September moon I invite you to focus on Preparation. What does the energy of Preparation mean for you? The energy flow of the September moon is of clearing out the clutter, settling in and paying deeper attention. Becoming slower and preparing for the colder months to come.

September

The grain harvest is in, and the fruit and vegetable harvest is starting to follow. The days are still warm but it's turning cooler at night which turns into misty mornings. As the children return to school you can feel the turn of the year in the air. The rhythm of the land is changing.

This is the point of time where we are starting to think about what we're going to do in the Winter, what we're going to do in the dark. For some of us that may mean needing to think about being careful with energy and about putting in place self-care. So many of us are affected by Seasonal Affective Disorder as the warmth and the light slips away and the days become shorter.

Modern living has us functioning 24/7 with artificial light and many of us will travel to and from work in the dark as the year turns. So now is the time to be thinking about what preparation you need to make for yourself to help you get through the darker months, they come round faster than we realise and can catch us by surprise.

It's also thinking about what have you harvested so far this Autumn? Or what are you anticipating harvesting?

What did you begin in the Spring, what did you nurture through Summer, what is coming to fruit for you now?

In nature the plants are preparing their seeds for the next cycle, now that their growth is nearly over for the year. The seeds will fall to the ground and rest through the dark till the Spring. What do you need to allow to fall to the ground and let rest in the dark for the next cycle?

It's time now for a slower energy, but creative, more spacious. To centre into the routine of Autumn, around school if you have children or are studying yourself. To allow for slower days and prepare for those shorter days of Winter. To anticipate the coming of Christmas and the demands that will ask of us.

We may not want to be going out quite so much and are wanting to nestle in at home more and more. This is a good time to write letters or make phone calls or Skype. Make more time to reach out to people around us or invite people into our homes and share. Share harvest, share hospitality, the good old tradition of the harvest festival and sharing the surplus with those in need. That may mean literally food or it might mean time and attention.

A time to think about sharing our abundance with one another. A time to think about our communities, friends and neighbours. A time for centring and grounding, focusing in on what really matters.

Preparation

Keeping Warm

Unearth your woolly jumpers and put favourite blankets near to the places where you spend time at home, they can be pulled over knees and around shoulders as the evenings get chillier or when you want to step out into the garden on those cool, misty mornings.

Nourishment

Stock up the larder with the makings for good, warming foods. Pulses and grains for stews and soups to be made with seasonal vegetables. Keep a stock of yummy jams to be eaten on hot toast or crumpets. Food can be a great comfort as the weather gets colder, have some treats, but take care of your body too!

Diary Management

Look ahead in your diary a bit, Christmas isn't that far away. Who do you need to make time to see? Are there parties coming up? Make sure you schedule in down time as well. Try and find a balance of time and energy through the Autumn as the year gets slower and darker, otherwise you will arrive into the festive period exhausted and not able to enjoy it.

Write/Journal/Paint

I imagine....

I am prepared for....

How will you journey into Winter...?

THE OCTOBER MOON

Hunter's Moon, Blood Moon, Sanguine Moon,
Falling Leaf Moon, Shedding Moon

For the cycle of the October moon I invite you to focus
on Honouring. What does the energy of Honouring
mean for you? The energy flow of the October moon is
of deepening, darkening and releasing before the turn
of the year.

OCTOBER

Hunter's moon and theme for this month is honouring and remembering. Making space in the quieter times to think of that which matters.

We are in a space of honouring the land. This is the final harvest and we're honouring and giving thanks for everything that we've harvested as we prepare to go into the Winter. You may be thinking about these preparations, about preserves and tinctures and essences.

Maybe thinking about firewood supplies and fluffy jumpers and soup recipes and then all these things are honouring. The jumper made by your grandmother, the soup recipe you got from your grandfather. Those traditions and gifts passed down by those who have gone before us and we are honouring them when we use these things.

Perhaps you are preparing for Halloween. Although it has become very commercial in this century there are honouring traditions still woven through it. I was taught that you put a pumpkin in the window with the scary face turned outwards. This had two purposes, the light was for the ancestors, for those who were gone so that they would know we were thinking about them and then scary face was to keep out any energies that we didn't want to come into the house.

In some spiritual traditions Halloween (or Samhain) is regarded as New Year and the start of a new cycle of the wheel of the year. This can be a good time to set intentions for the coming year, to root them in the dark and ask the blessing of the ancestors.

Think about what you might want to release and leave behind in the year that is gone. Then think about what you are grateful for? What do you want to carry forward? This is a great time to do a vision board, collecting pictures and words from magazines and creating a visual of the energies and dreams for the year to come.

The land has given us her gifts and we are grateful, we are prepared for the Winter dark with the comforts and healing of her gifts. We can show our thanks, give her honour by giving something back. Feeding the birds and wild animals (please check with wildlife charities for the right foods), preparing gardens and allotments for Winter or by donating to work that honours and protects the land.

We remember our ancestors, we remember those who are gone, we show them they are not forgotten. Honouring them, honouring ourselves. Giving thanks for all that we are, stepping forward with our ancestors at our backs, moving strongly in truth and power, resting in the dark months for renewal in the Spring.

Honouring

Offering

This is a time to make offerings to the land and the ancestors. What those offerings are will vary depending on intent and purpose. They may be physical items including food or drink, or it might be drumming, poetry or music. Using sound is a really simple way of honouring person or place and you don't need any tools.

Litter Picking

One of the most powerful ways you can honour this land that we live on is by collecting litter. Keep a bag (and maybe gloves) with you everywhere you go and pick up rubbish that you find

Empty Chair

This is an honouring that is typically connected to Halloween but can be done at other times where it feels appropriate. The idea being that when you feast you leave a chair empty as a place for your beloved dead. This shows them they are welcome and not forgotten. An alternative option is to light a candle and place it on the table or nearby family activities.

WRITE/JOURNAL/PAINT

I honour....

I am making space for....

What do ancestors mean for you?

THE NOVEMBER MOON

Dark Moon, Snow Moon, Frost Moon, Beaver Moon,
Mourning Moon, Tree Moon, Fog Moon

For the cycle of the November moon I invite you to focus on Cleansing. What does the energy of Cleansing mean for you? The energy flow of the November moon is of letting go of what is past, clearing the way for the new season to come

November

We're coming into Winter quite firmly now and we're thinking about clearing the way of anything that we don't want to take into the deepest of the dark with us. This moon is a good time to review all that has gone before you this year and make sure you clear out anything that might be in your way, metaphorically or literally.

Our brains and bodies have forgotten about how to live properly with light and dark because we have artificial light. A few generations ago we would have finished our harvests last month and we would now be preparing the stores ready for the Winter. We would be settling in for the longer, darker nights. Sitting around a fire, singing and storytelling. All the things that there isn't the time for in the Spring and Summer and Autumn, when the land demands to be planted and tended and harvested. The Winter was the time of rest, but we don't live like that anymore. But something in us remembers and yearns for it.

Our lives are plugged in constantly 24/7 and we're not really designed to live like that. We all desperately need to unplug and rediscover the dark and the quiet. Once upon a time, not really that long ago we would have had a community around us to support us with our stuff. But many of us have exchanged real life people and community for connection with an electronic, online world. When it's cold and dark outside and there is no community fire to join, it's easy to snuggle up in bed and switch on social media and get that positive feedback through the screen.

It's really important to try and unplug sometimes, even if it's just for short periods. To take time to notice the energies of the earth and to tune into the moon.

Transformation happens within the dark, like the seed that evolves in the deep earth. Time to release, to let go, to say goodbye to all that no longer serves or heals you. Leave behind those things which will hold you back. Cleanse and clear the way for a new you to emerge with the return of the light in the Spring.

It is time to rest now, to reflect, to curl up in the warmth and centre yourself with creature comforts. What has to come to pass for you this year? What has not? What can you dream into being for yourself through these dark, quiet months of Winter? Who will you be when you emerge?

Cleansing

Sacred Smoke

Throughout the world many cultures have used the burning of herbs to create a sacred smoke to cleanse the air and the energy field of a place or person. Use this practice to keep the energies of your home and self clear.

Water

Water is life and has the most powerful cleansing energies. If you can bear the cold, dipping your feet (or whole self if you can stand it!) into rivers or seas can be hugely cleansing. But a shower or bath at home will do and save the wild water for warmer days. Ask the water to take away all that you wish to let go of, feel yourself refreshed and renewed.

Digital Detox

Make space in your life without technology. Whether that's just an hour without your mobile phone or persuading the whole family to go off grid for a day a week and all going without any tech for entertainment. Or maybe something between the two. See what works and feels good to you. But make space to connect with the world without a screen.

WRITE/JOURNAL/PAINT

I am releasing....

I clear the way for....

I dream....

THE DECEMBER MOON

Long Night Moon, Full Cold Moon, Wolf Moon,
Oak Moon, Big Winter Moon

For the cycle of the December moon I invite you to focus on Strength. What does the energy of Strength mean for you? The energy flow of the December moon is of deep rest in the dark, hibernation, connection and waiting for the return of the light.

December

So here it is, the darkest point of the year, coming towards the longest night at Winter Solstice, where we all hope for the return of the sun. Knowing that when it has passed, the light will slowly but surely return to us, ready to begin the cycle of the year all over again.

This can be a hard time on everyone, it's dark and often cold and wet and yet there is a certain comfort of snuggling up indoors, shutting the dark out behind the curtains for a while. As the festive season comes round and the houses start to shine with lights, we are reminded that the light will return and there is joy to be found in the dark.

The trick is to not succumb to stuff to make yourself feel better, the media and the shops use our vulnerability of the season to encourage us to buy, buy, buy to keep the darkness at bay. But shopping and consumption has a very short lived effect. There is a strength in resisting the tidal wave of stuff and lights and noise at this time of year, to hold steadfast at the centre of it all and to find your own path and meaning amongst it all.

Our ancestors knew they could not wilfully overconsume so early in the Winter, that the stores of the harvest had to last for some months yet to come. That didn't stop them from celebrating, but it was centred around family and community and connection. It was about creating pockets of joy in the cold and dark times, to lead each other towards Spring with hope and love.

The energy at this time of year can be relentless, an endless round of parties and school events and socialising. In a way that is often at odds with how the cold and dark is making us feel. One of the best ways I have ever found of maintaining my strength and resilience at this time of year, is to go to bed early with a cup of tea and a good book!

This should be a time to deepen into ourselves, into our communities and into our spiritual practices. To take strength from them to see us through to the light on the other side. For the moon will turn again and so will the year and the light will return.

The time to rest has come, you've worked hard all year, sowing, tending and harvesting. Time to rest now. In the dark, the deep quiet. Time to gather your strength, to tend to your inner resources. To look within and tend your inner fires.

Look back a little, see the year gone by. How far have you come? What's changed? What hasn't? Look forward a little. What are you seeking? What is waiting for you? What do you need to do to get to where you want to be?

Strength

Fitness

Are you as fit and strong as you would like to be? What could you begin, however small to work towards being physically stronger? It can be as simple as a series of stretches and a good walk outdoors or you can really go for it and get down the gym. Start small and build up and don't give yourself a hard time about it!

Emotional Strength

How do you maintain your emotional resilience? Have you been tending to it? Now is a good time to pick up the phone to a best friend, to arrange a supper night out at the pub or host people at home. Maybe you need a bit more and it's time to book that appointment with a therapist or life coach and really look at what is underneath.

Silence

Scientists have confirmed that silence is vital to human wellbeing and yet we live in a world saturated with noise. To the point that many of us find silence uncomfortable. Try heading for the woods, turn your phone off and let the silence in. Find strength in peace and quiet.

Write/Journal/Paint

I feel strong when....

I am diving deeply into....

My Winter dream is....

Summary

It is possible to create real transformation in your life by bringing yourself into alignment with your Natal Moon Phase Cycle. If you are willing to take the time to follow the moon and notice what is happening within you at each phase, you can find ease, growth and stability in all areas of your life.

You may also find that you have a cycle that runs with the seasons of the year as well. Perhaps by following some of the suggested actions and creative prompts in this book you will find new ways of being and creating that you hadn't thought about before.

The key thing is to pay attention, to maintain that attention and learn to be in relationship with your own cycle, then you will truly be living Moon Wise.

ONCE IN A BLUE MOON

It may have come to your attention that most years we have thirteen full moons in a calendar year, but my moon cycle year only has twelve in it. The thirteenth moon in a year is called a blue moon and there is a whole host of myth and folklore around the meaning of it. It doesn't happen every year and typically happens in January or March because of February being a short month. It happens due to the changes in the calendar that happened in 1752 which moved everything by 10 days.

In terms of living Moon Wise, I have found the most helpful thing to do is to look at the year as a whole when there are thirteen moons in it and work out which one seems to be the odd one out. This is entirely intuitive, there is no rule of thumb here. But if you follow my thoughts on the energies of each moon cycle in this book, you should be able to get a sense of where the extra moon doesn't fit. It will be the one which doesn't seem to fit the energy of the month it is in, it will feel like it's out of place. It's very hard to explain this, you can only explore it for yourself.

Of course this is the problem with trying to fit a moon calendar into the calendar of months! Modern magical practice offers a Blue Moon as an opportunity to add extra juice to your work. In terms of living Moon Wise I think you probably need to see what arises for you in terms of your personal cycle, rather than any outer ideas about what it might mean or represent. For those of you who are dark moon born, you're not going to appreciate the extra fullness!

The phrase 'once in a blue moon' is used now to mean something that rarely or never happens. But actually the first reference to a blue moon comes from a proverb recorded in 1528.

> *If they say the moon is blue,*
> *We must believe that it is true.*

So in fact once upon a time, saying the moon was blue was actually a reference to something being quite absurd!

Of course we also occasionally get two new moons in a calendar month and these extra ones are referred to as Black Moons. Like a blue moon there is a host of lore attached to it which suggests that it is a time of additional power. If your full moon born, you may not agree!

RESOURCES

There are Natal Moon Birth Charts and downloadable moon cycle charts available at www.awenclement.com

Books About Working With the Moon

Moon Magic by Lori Reid
Moon Magic by Rachel Patterson
Moon Time: The Art of Harmony with Nature and Lunar Cycles by Johanna Paugger and Thomas Poppe

Books about Menstruation and Fertility

Moon Time by Lucy Pearce
Menarche: A Journey to Womanhood by Rachel Hertogs
Thirteen Moons: A Cycle Charting Journey by Jane Hardwicke Collings
Ten Moons: The Inner Journey of Pregnancy by Jane Hardwicke Collings

Diaries and Calendars

Earth Pathways Diary and Calendar
We'Moon Diary and Calendar

KEEP IN TOUCH

I hope you have enjoyed learning about how to live Moon Wise. I hope it gives you the clarity it has given me.

Need more help? Do you want to join me? Here's how!

- Join me on a Moon Wise Retreat
- Have a Moon Wise Healing Session
- Join my Moon Wise Facebook group

www.awenclement.com

Share your Moon Wise stories with me. I'd love to hear from you.

Email them to:

awen@wildmagpie.co.uk

Bright Moon Blessings

Awen

Printed in Great Britain
by Amazon

82403461R00072